TITANIA'S · CRYSTAL BALL

TITANIA HARDIE

CONNECTIONS
BOOK PUBLISHING

For my mother,
with her all-seeing hazel eyes.

A CONNECTIONS EDITION
This edition published in Great Britain in 2003 by
Connections Book Publishing Limited
St Chad's House, 148 King's Cross Road,
London WC1X 9DH

Text copyright © Titania Hardie 2003
Illustration copyright © Nanette Hoogslag 2003
This edition copyright © Eddison Sadd Editions 2003

British Library Cataloguing-in-Publication data available on request.

ISBN: 978-1-85906-139-8

11 13 14 12 10

Phototypeset in Bernhard Modern BT using QuarkXPress on Apple Macintosh
Origination by Rainbow
Printed and manufactured in China by Nordica International Ltd, Hong Kong

Contents

Introduction

ONE OF THE MOST EVOCATIVE IMAGES in the whole genre of mind, body and spirit subjects – and of mysticism itself – is that of the gifted seer contemplating the depths of a crystal ball. These 'enchantresses' (though there have been male crystal gazers, too) have been bequeathed to our collective imaginations in a number of guises: painted by Pre-Raphaelite artists as beautiful, enigmatic femmes fatales, or described vividly in the myth and crystal lore of Arthurian derivation, or simply suggesting myriad possibilities to us from our own experiences of the gypsy fortune-teller at a fair. There is something magical, perhaps even poetic, about the dream world which may be unlocked for us in a beautiful crystal sphere!

In this little book, and with this beautiful moon-like object, we will be looking at the history of crystalomancy – the technical name for crystal ball gazing. We will look at how it developed from the use of watery surfaces and reflective objects, and see how to use the ball to develop our clairvoyant capacities and our 'third eye'. We need to understand what is actually happening in the glass itself, consider the relationship of the crystal ball to the moon – the planet of our subconscious understanding – and we will look at the optimum times for using the ball, and the symbolic language through which it communicates with us. Given the right preparation and focus, it is our lens on a new vision of the world – literally, a chance to see the world through rose-coloured glass. We can then think about other ways of using the ball, and allow it to usher us into healing and positive creative energies. It is an exciting journey to make.

You might like to handle your new crystal ball gently and intimately as you read (though be careful not to scratch it). This will help to infuse your own personality into it as you think, and learn, and become acquainted with the concepts of this lovely tool. Take your time, and allow yourself plenty of relaxed privacy. As you do so, the ball will become a personalized tool for you alone – like an artist awakening the signature elements of a much-loved pen. Soon, you will understand it perfectly, and have many extraordinary hours of pleasure and knowledge with it. Let us begin …

Chapter 1

What is 'crystalomancy'?

Pronounced as 'CRYSTAL' is normally pronounced, with the emphasis then on 'o' as in 'orange' and 'mancy' so that it sounds like '**ge**og**raphy**', this complex-seeming word refers to a straightforward activity. Crystalomancy is one of the most ancient forms of 'scrying' – looking into crystal. Scrying itself is the act of divination, coming from the word 'descry', or discern dimly.

CRYSTAL-GAZING THROUGH THE AGES

We know that crystalomancy existed in early Christian times, but it seems to have originated much earlier – possibly in the Kabala (the ancient branch of occult learning from the tradition of Jewish mysticism). The Egyptians also scried with crystal and large precious stones, regarding the wonderful little spheres (especially large rock crystals) as the Eye of Horus. In Classical Greek mythology, three sisters called the Grææ (meaning 'the Old Ones') passed between them one eye, giving them second sight. This was a crystal eye, and was borrowed by Perseus as he sought the home of the Medusa. The activity of scrying with either a crystal or, indeed, the surface of a lake, or ink, or other shiny stones, has also been practised in one form or another by the aborigines of Australia, the American Indians and the Mayan and Incan inhabitants of South America. A crystal sphere was also found in the cave at Wookey Hole, near my home in Somerset, in England, along with other objects used traditionally in witchcraft, suggesting that this cave was, indeed, the abode of one of Britain's earliest known witches. In more modern times, Dr Dee, who was the celebrated astrologer to Queen Elizabeth I, consulted a crystal ball to flesh out his prophecies with more significant visions; and Nostradamus is said to have used a crystal, likewise to assist in his astrological calculations and predictions.

HOW MIGHT IT WORK?

Crystals and other reflective surfaces are employed for two reasons. Principally, the effect of the shine is to give a sense of 'white out' to our normal vision, encouraging us to look beyond the obvious with the naked eye. This idea will be familiar to anyone who has successfully focused on the 'magic eye' pictures, which effectively ask us to look *through* them to identify a three-dimensional image. A reflective surface encourages our vision to work in a similar way – ignoring the obvious superficial picture so that we may see more clearly by looking through it. These objects are most successfully looked at in soft, minimal light and, traditionally, by moonlight. This brings us to the second reason why crystals, in particular, are such responsive objects for scrying and determining visions.

Crystals, milky gems like opals and moonstones, lakes – indeed, all bodies of water – and reflective items like mirrors all have a strong affinity with the moon, which is the patron of reflection through its own relationship with the sun. The moon is also emblematic of our feminine, creative, intuitive side; it governs the realms of our dreams and our imagination. It rules the earth's tides and our emotional, receptive states and, as our bodies are made up of such a high percentage of fluid, we are all powerfully influenced by it. Working in harmony with the moon assures success in magic making and clairvoyant ritual: our emotions, feelings and personal powers of magnetism are quantifiable throughout the moon's phases. At full moon, our feelings are highly sensitized. I will discuss, in the pages ahead, the importance of using the moon's rhythms to help us gaze into our ball most effectively.

But for now, it is significant to understand that the ball itself is ruled by the moon. Crystals as a whole come under her dominion, and the structure of rock crystal has a long tradition of use in altering the physical and mental state and changing energy frequency – a property that has been deployed in the use of crystal in radio sets and watches. Rock crystal – and the many other varied types of crystal – has the propensity to affect our own energies and receptivity. As it does this, it alters our own frequency and allows us to become more like radio sets ourselves – receptive to waves, thoughts and images that would other-wise be out of our vision. The Australian Aborigines have respected the use of crystals – and other shiny stones – in the same way, to propel the consciousness beyond apparent time, using them also as an aid to telepathy and sending messages to others at a distance.

Many people subscribe to the theory that only a pure, Mother-Earth-grown rock crystal is appropriate for gazing; however, rock crys-tals of any substantial size are both highly prized and highly priced! The crystal sphere that you have to work with here is beautiful pure optical glass, which I believe has a number of advantages. The first is that it is clear – fractures and flaws are almost inevitable in earth crystal, and these can be both distracting and confusing, obstructing the visions just as they begin to flow for you. The other advantage is that pure glass, often called 'crystal', is itself in a permanent liquid state – glass is never solid, always moving, even in great stained-glass windows. This gives it strong connections with the moon, and with the idea that the world – and our experience of it – is never static, but always evolving. This is sympathetic to the fluidity of the visions themselves. Finally, the shine of this quite perfect, high quality glass is ideal for capturing reflections. This suggests a correlation with the oracles of the springs in Celtic and Greek tradition – as though there is a well-spring at the heart of the crystal ball itself. So, think of this crystal ball as a new optical lens, through which to see a new world – like putting on special glasses.

BECOMING CLAIRVOYANT

The properties of your crystal ball, and the self-discipline you will gain in learning to read it, will result in your own, internal 'seeing eye', which is traditionally called the 'third eye', and is located at a major chakra point in the middle of your forehead, almost between the eyes. You will achieve this, in part, as the exercises to help you 'see' and focus on the crystal ball encourage your natural psychic propensities, or your 'sixth sense', to grow. Research has shown that at least one in two men are telepathic or receptive, and perhaps more than two in every three women – either because we are closer to the moon, or less inclined to try to rationalize the messages we are given intuitively, or even perhaps because, historically, we have had so much practice at inferring information and achieving understanding instinctively from the relatively little that our gender was told! This was once a vital part of our survival – our instincts had to be sharper and our senses of smell, touch and taste were more sensitive, in a world where there were more obvious perils, and life seemed more transient. Survival depended on the sharpness and focus of every instinct and sensory capacity.

With exercise, we can control and direct these often unsolicited telepathic messages more frequently, and to greater effect. I like to think that our amazing brains are like the most complex computers — capable of quite astonishing, synchronizing feats; but without instructions, we don't seem to understand how to utilize them fully. Moreover, mobile phones and modern electronic retrieval methods have made the need for picking up other 'thought waves' a relatively obsolete skill. The use of your crystal ball will exercise your 'flabby' psychic muscle.

One of the most interesting things about using a crystal ball is that our ordinary visual and aural abilities are sharpened — we are effectively making ourselves more clair**voyant** (able to see pictures) or clair**audient** (able to hear messages), depending on which is our stronger sense. (I will speak a little in the next chapter about the differences between being clairvoyant and clairaudient.) In either case, the ball will help you to develop your visual senses, and it will admit voices — or sounds — to those who naturally work with auditory skill. This means that all of your intuitive skills — whether you use them to read tarot or work magic ritual, or simply depend on them quietly in everyday business and domestic decisions — will have greater depth and elasticity. The use of the crystal ball will even bolster your visual gifts, and you will start to see everything around you in more detail, and with living technicolour.

Chapter 2

What will happen in the crystal ball?

THERE ARE MANY VIEWS about what is manifesting when you look into a crystal ball. For those who are inclined to look at the issue from a practical standpoint, it might be that the crystal ball is a trigger that helps us to access our complex unconscious state, and reach into the ideas and receptivity we don't normally concentrate on – those thoughts that lie below the surface of our more banal and practical lives. You might think of this as being akin to a self-induced, but vividly recalled, hypnotic state, which gives us access to the subtlest information. In a sense, this is strongly related to dream vision, although dreams tend to come to us unbidden, whereas scrying in a crystal is a willing decision to tune into our subconscious inner voices. Many people, however, who are very close to their psychic gifts, make it a practice to instruct their dreams to contemplate important issues, so that on waking, clear answers and new understandings have been found. This is something that my mother has always done, and she is accomplished at directing this subconscious information in her dreams. In this way, crystal ball gazing bears a close relationship with this kind of inner-voiced information.

An extension of this view is that the crystal itself – whether it is a genuine rock crystal or a laboratory-grown crystal, or the glass crystal sphere we are working with here – enables us to tap into its own special and unique properties and turn us into individual radio sets. Certainly, if you have ever seen how rays of light are altered as they enter crystal, and the way glass and crystal prisms break the spectrum into the rainbow, you will appreciate the idea that your own visions and thought waves can undergo this kind of transformation. The mind is able, thus, to reproduce the interesting images from the inner mind, almost like watching a small television screen in the glass. These images have a scientific name: eidetic images. They are perfectly real and utterly quantifiable to those who see them in this way (many children do, for instance). The poet William Blake was alleged to perceive eidetic images very regularly, throughout his life, to the bemusement of friends who watched him sketching angels, moving his head and line of sight to see them three-dimensionally.

For some other people, the images are thought to be transferred telepathically, either from the mind of someone you are reading for, or from the mind and magnetic field of somebody you are concentrating on in order to access information about them or concerning them. It may be possible, in this way, to pick up images and fragments of others' thoughts, and even conversations — especially if you are more clairaudient, of which I will say more below. In either case, the crystal acts like a transmitter. It should be needless to say that this kind of scrying demands integrity on the part of the gazer; if you pick up your visions in this way you must direct and focus your own mind in a manner that respects others' privacy. But, again, I will say a little more about this later.

The most psychic individuals may experience a variant of these concepts, picking up really clairvoyant images and information in a variety of ways. This happens for some people quite freely, and the information they literally see in the glass appears to come from nowhere. It is still working in the manner discussed above, with the crystal acting as both a self-hypnotic focusing tool and a miniature radio set, but many people do appear to have a natural affinity for crystal gazing, and find that images, colours and, ultimately, quite complex scenes seem to be enacted in the sphere without any effort. If this applies to you, you may feel that the information is coming from a close relationship with spirit guides. Many gifted clairvoyants, psychics and healers work wonderfully in tandem with spirit presences, and the ball may help to further communication with your own spiritual guides and subsequently strengthen your intuitions in everyday matters. Certainly, many people who work regularly with crystal balls feel calm and more centred through using them.

IS THERE ANYTHING IN THE CRYSTAL THAT SHOULD FRIGHTEN ME?

As long as you remain positive and calm, there is no need to worry that the ball will manifest 'bad spirits'. Many people do believe in negative spirits, and I wouldn't deny that for them these negative presences are very real. Nor would I suggest that this idea is wrong: we all experience things psychically in different ways. My own belief is that negative entities are brought forth from the fearful recesses of our own subconscious minds, which can be very powerful and destructive. If our personal experience of spirit presences is troubling, then we probably have deep-seated worries about something unresolved. It is often the most sensitive souls who experience this: I for one never watch horror movies, as I believe (laugh at me by all means) that they bother my inner sanctity at a subliminal level. You may be immune to this kind of auto-suggestion (lucky you!), but if you are highly imaginative with a strong mental power to envisage things clearly with your mind's eye, it may be best to concentrate on positive and powerfully radiant ideas. Call it positive thinking, if you like, but I believe it works in all the things we do, and it will work in your crystal gazing. Keep your mind calm and clear, and positive and hopeful, and you need not worry about 'gremlins' in the glass.

This isn't to say there won't be times when the visions in your glass will show flashes of troubling images that seem to be about sad news or events. As human beings, we do experience a mixture of good and bad in the high and low rhythms that make up our lives. Sometimes, bad news is inevitable. However, if you remain positive minded, it is likely that images or information you access can be preventative. In this way, if you are not afraid but look honestly in the face of challenges, your crystal should be able to help you to be forewarned, and thus fore-armed. It may be wise, though, not to gaze on occasions when you are very tired, not well, or depressed. In such instances, your own positive thoughts are hindered, and the glass may not assuage these negative ideas. Put the glass away until you feel your pulse beating strongly again.

CLAIRVOYANT OR CLAIRAUDIENT – WHICH ARE YOU?

Once you start gazing at your crystal, you will soon become aware of the way the ball works for you. Some of you will experience visions inside the glass, whereas others will see them in the light-play around the crystal; some of you may see symbolic visions more on the surface of the ball, whereas others will find that it is almost speaking to you, with sounds as much a part of what you receive as picture images.

How your information manifests has much to do with the individual strengths you have been developing since your childhood. Musical people who hear subtle inflections in voices, and distinguish frequencies and noises that many people miss, are likely to develop a clairaudient approach to their psychic skills. If this describes your sensitivities, you may find that you literally begin to hear words and sounds as you hold the ball and gaze into it. You might hear birds or the sea, or traffic noises or snatches of music. You are effectively being told psychic information, and the crystal ball is acting as a kind of radio transmitter. With this may come a visual impression of colours and shapes, and the capacity to see these will grow sharper with practice.

But, perhaps you are more of a natural artist – the kind of person who remembers exactly the shade of blue someone was wearing (my daughter is like this), or who has a perfect and vivid recall of a friend's house decoration. Usually, someone whose visual sense is this highly developed will be able to draw objects and faces from recall alone. If this sounds like a description of your talents, the crystal is likely to offer you very clear, detailed pictures that, again, will grow more distinct with use.

For both clairaudients (like my mother and me) and clairvoyants (like my daughter and sister), images may appear in various ways. You might see little enactments of past or future events. At times, we dream and scry symbolically, so that our subconscious speaks to us through a referential language of signs. This is an adventure, opening up your sensitivities to manifold understandings. But it can also be quite complex, since symbols can be interpreted in different ways. In the pages ahead, we will consider ways in which you might find meaning for yourself.

We are now ready to prepare our crystal for use, and set the scene ...

Chapter 3

The relaxed mind
and the tranquil space

IN YOUR FIRST EXPERIMENTS with crystal gazing, be aware that certain times give you optimum receptivity and psychic awareness, and it's a good idea to be unhurried in your approach. We have already mentioned the importance of the moon – how her tides affect our emotions and feelings – and as crystal gazing comes under her aegis, you should try to work with an understanding of the moon's phases, especially while you are getting started. Good initial results will give you the encouragement to persevere.

It is also really helpful to create a comfortable scrying environment. You are going to turn yourself into a radio receiver (or a human television perhaps), and you definitely don't want 'interference' to affect the transmitted waves! A few minimal props will help, and it may take some time and practice to find out exactly what works best for you. Here are some basic steps that will help you create a calm and productive work space.

1. Choose the best time:

⚙ Scrying on a **waxing moon** (when it is growing from new towards full) will probably give you a more personal feeling of energy and intuition than working on a waning moon. We are more in tune with ourselves the nearer we get to the moon being full; our emotions and awarenesses are at a peak. On the night of a beautiful full moon itself, our senses are at full throttle, which is why so many people go a little mad at this time! This can be very productive for crystal gazing, as your brimming senses are more likely to pick up on the electro-magnetic thoughts and impulses of others.

✵ **Night-time** has traditionally been considered to be more conducive to crystal gazing than day-time. Apart from the obvious idea that it is the moon's time, this is because thoughts, noise, traffic and people's lives generally slow down at night (although not always of course); it is definitely best to pick a time when you have some tranquillity in your own mind. If you are less hurried at night, and less likely to be phoned or have a visitor drop by, then night is right for you. Certainly, the thoughts of others (who may be part of the circle who will influence events around you) are more often in stand-by mode at night; and the closer to sleep time, the better. If you, however, are lucky enough to have calm and a little privacy during the day, that's fine. You may pick up some interesting things at this time, when the world around you is more business oriented. Sunrise is also an opportune time to gaze: the start of a new day, when the early light is quite ethereal. You might like to try this, at least occasionally.

2. Prepare your space to aid meditation:

- ☼ The room in which you will keep your crystal ball should be clean and comfortable. If you wish, use incense or oil burners to activate your sense of **smell**. Scents that aid psychic concentration include benzoin, frankincense, patchouli, myrrh and sandalwood; whereas rose, pine, lavender or basil have a purifying quality. Make sure you choose something you like, which will not give you a headache.

- ☼ If you like **music** and find it helps you become contemplative and relaxed, then choose something soft and unobtrusive. Meditative choruses such as plainsong church music work well, as does classical music. If you are used to having massages with rainforest or dolphin noises and this induces calm for you, you might select this. If you prefer silence, that's fine. The idea of sound is that it either helps you to become slightly self-hypnotized and sensitive or to relax, but if it does neither of these things for you, omit it.

- ☼ It is important to obtain the right degree of **light**. Whichever time of day you choose to use your crystal ball, your room should have a good balance between being slightly cloistered and private, and admitting a feeling of some openness, to allow your mind to become expansive. This is best achieved by having some fresh air (but not too much draught), a room of sufficient size not to feel claustrophobic, and most importantly by creating a special feeling with the light. It is traditional to scry by moon- or candle-light. Watch the position of your candles if you have a window open, but you would ideally achieve a soft, reflective glow of just the candles in the sphere, so that wondrous shards of light bounce off the ball. Five candles are traditionally employed around the ball, to represent the five senses, and the ball itself transcends those five to become the focus of the sixth sense. If you suffer from the effects of strobe lighting in any way, you should use a much softer light source, such as a steady lamp at a distance.

⊛ If you perceive yourself as a tactile, touchy-feely person (as I do), the sense of **touch** may be especially significant for you. Give your ball a tactile cloth to rest on, such as chenille, velvet or silk; it will subtly captivate the mind's eye and allow you to perceive visions that have an extra, almost tactile dimension in them. It may also add to your personal feeling of comfort and tranquillity to sit on a soft suede or velvet cushion to gaze. Choose what excites you and is convenient: but above all, be comfortable.

⊛ Sense of taste rarely comes into scrying. However, ideally **all your senses** should be active, so you may like to begin your session with something on your palate to stimulate your taste buds. Choose anything from chocolate to a citrus-flavoured sweet; several people I know like to crystal gaze with cardamom sweets or pods, or chew on a basil or mint leaf for a moment at the start. There is no requirement on this one, though.

3. Basic props:

✪ You will need to make sure your crystal ball won't roll around. You could use the lovely **stand** that is included in the pack, or you might wish to create one of your own. It is nice to make whatever it is you will use, yourself, to personalize your crystal. A simple stand could be made from strong card covered in a fabric you like. You might embroider something special. Or you could use the stand provided, with a special under-cloth to personalize it.

✪ You will need some form of **cloth** as mentioned under 'touch', above. It is traditional to lay either a black or a white cloth under the ball, either of silk or velvet. When you have finished gazing, you might wish to wrap the ball back up in this cloth, to keep it clean and protected, as well as to store its personal energies – which will accumulate.

✪ You need either candles (place them safely in votive holders or tea-light glasses, and put them on a suitable surface) or another **soft**

light source such as a low-wattage lamp. If you are very lucky, you might be able to position the ball to catch the light of a bright, full moon with no other light source; but this will only happen on a few nights throughout the year. If you are using candles, always respect draughts, and take care to be candle safe.

✦ Keep a **notebook** for writing down a few keywords during your scrying session. It is best to write this up in more detail afterwards, in a crystal diary (I will speak about this in the final chapter), but to avoid interrupting the flow, a small notepad will enable you to record a word or two to trigger more memory at your leisure.

PURIFYING AND PERSONALIZING YOUR CRYSTAL BALL

Do this after all else is set in place. Hopefully, you have been reading this book while gently handling your sphere and considering the ideas of crystalomancy. Now, before your first reading, 'magnetize' it in the following way.

1. For first use, wash your crystal ball in a mild solution of triple-milled rose soap and warm water. Place a cloth on the bottom of the bowl so you don't scratch the ball. As you wash it, ask that it becomes a lens on your world, and that it provides you with new insights and visions.

2. Rinse the ball in a flower-water solution. Rose water or orange-flower water are ideal; or you may prefer to follow the tradition of using vinegar and water. You might like to get a small bottle of special scented vinegar for this.

3. Dry the ball in a lint-free cloth (such as a linen tea towel), and then polish it up with a special cloth for glass. Once you have these items, you might like to keep them just for your crystal.

4. Finally, wrap the crystal in the cloth you will use as the backdrop, and pass it through either the scented stream from your incense or oil burner if you are using these, or simply above a lit candle (a scented one would be very appropriate). As you do this, dedicate your crystal ball:

5. With these words you are directing your crystal's energy, and connecting with it yourself. Say something of your own creation, along the lines of: 'I dedicate this crystal to greater vision and understanding; I promise to use it wisely, and not to harm others with careless words and half-formed thoughts; I will contemplate my information with humility, and strive to be of help wherever possible. So mote it be.' (But do, please, say something like this in your own words, for it is *your* ritual alone.)

So now, shall we start looking ...?

Chapter 4

The world through rose-tinted glass

Now THAT YOU HAVE CLEANSED your crystal and prepared your space and yourself, you are ready to gaze.

Once your lighting is arranged, look at your crystal ball for a few moments, very intently. Breathe deeply, in a relaxed way, and try to feel the rhythm of your breath entering into the crystal itself. Pick it up carefully and warm it in your hands, while you look right through to the centre of the ball: you may see several things in the real world reflected in it, and the images may be reversed, as in a camera lens. Now you may replace it to sit independently on its cloth or stand.

Close your eyes and see the globe in your mind's eye for a moment; then reopen your eyes, and begin to gaze at the ball in proper concentration. Look deeply into the spherical shape. Don't try too hard to see anything (strange as that sounds!); your goal for the first few times is to try to get your eyes to look *through* the ball, so that you are inviting your mind and perceptions to elude the physical nature of the ball, and to gain a oneness with the light that seems to come from within it. Don't hurry this – take your time. En route to finding the inner being of the crystal ball in itself, you may find a particular area within it that draws you. If so, concentrate your attention on that part. It may be, too, that you feel a spirit within the ball – a sort of elfin presence. This will be especially true if you are someone who is conscious of having spirit guides around you in your life. But, if you don't experience that, it really doesn't matter. *Your* ball will speak to *you*; it is *your* organ of extra sight. Be prepared to give the relationship between you the time it needs in order to grow. Remember that, the more dominant a personality you are, the harder it is to 'lose' yourself and let the ball do the talking. Many very strong people find it hard to let themselves go under hypnosis, too. Persevere gently. If you are still struggling on the third or fourth occasion, consider how you would perceive the images in a 'magic eye' picture by blurring your eyesight and looking right across the obvious images. Sooner or later, you will grasp it, but don't distress yourself if it takes a few attempts. I had to try six times before I could really see something properly in my first crystal ball — although I did feel as though I could hear the sea from the first; whereas my more visually-aware sister saw images dancing before her on her very first try!

FIRST VISIONS

After a while (it may be seconds or days, depending on your own response to the ball) the more clairvoyant among you may become aware of either a colour spreading over the ball, or a milky density, or even some play among the prisms of light which show you a few first visions. Colours and clouds are probably the most commonly experienced phenomena.

If you become aware of colours, first of all, enjoy the show! Do you have a feeling of the colour as uniform? Or is there a density in one area and a lighter shade towards the edges? Is the colour thick, or just misty? Does it resemble a cloud? Try to gain the most objective impression about your visions, and write down just a word to help you remember what the very first thing was you were aware of. The more you look, the more your own sight will seem to merge with the ball, so that eventually you will be unsure about where your real line of vision and that sparked by the crystal are separated.

If you don't see colour, you may yet see a kind of mistiness. This would suggest your crystal is clearing its voice, and is more likely to occur if you are the kind of person who is aware of spirits helping you. Take your time with this process. Relax into it and continue to breathe gently: you may soon receive much more complex images than most of us do to start with, in which case, the next chapter will be of more help.

Let us now consider the meaning of the colours – whether they are cloudy in formation, or filmy, or simply have a sense of changing lights. These colours should be perceived independently of the cloth you are using under your ball. If the cloth is white or dark, it will be fairly easy to see any departure from this colour-wise, but if your cloth is coloured, it will obviously influence the spectrum spreading over the globe itself.

COLOURS

- **White** You are experiencing a simple opening of the third eye – your first clairvoyant awareness with the crystal. White is, itself, an optimistic sight, and indicates a positivity about your present concerns. If your white is really quite a creamy cloudiness, this is a sign of good personal health and mental buoyancy, and also bodes well for your present life.

- **Pale yellow/gold** You are trying very hard! This colour is positive, representing the intellect and possibly the mental effort involved now in willing the crystal ball to talk to you. This is usual for the early sessions of gazing; but if your colour yellow persists so that you see it frequently, even after several appointments with your crystal ball, you might be concentrating on work a little bit too much. Make time to play more.

- **Rose** Always a welcome colour, rosy pink looks so pretty in the glass. If your first visions show rose, you are very much concerned with matters of the heart. If the colour looks strong and clear, this is a very good omen about your love life, and you could go on from here to ask questions about love, and see how the colour reacts. The stronger, brighter or prettier the shade, the better the outcome. If it dissipates a bit, you may be worrying too much.

✪ **Green** Any hue of green indicates that you are tired and your health is in need of some pampering. If this is only the first time you have scried, it may represent a tiredness borne of the eagerness to see something. If it persists, you need to look after yourself. If green appears quite brightly after a period when you have been ill, your body is doing its best to heal itself – good.

✪ **Blue** Shades of blue symbolize choices. Is it a sky blue? If so, you are feeling dreamy, but quite positive about issues in your life. Ask sky blue some mental questions, and see how the image responds. Any deepening of the colour suggests that you can proceed with your plans after very careful thought. If the blue is already a darker shade, you need to become a bit more positive in your thinking. You have important ideas on your mind, but you need to believe that you can break through and win. Blue, though, is a good colour in the glass.

✪ **Mauve/purple** This is a bonus. You are receiving affirmation that your psychic gifts are strengthening. You are also a very balanced person, with a good proportion of self-worth and generosity towards others. If the purple is very dark and cloud-like, you are, again, working too hard on your scrying. Try to relax a little and more visions will come. Purples are often the prelude to more exotic images and symbols.

- ✪ **Dark colours** These aren't simply bad, although they do indicate grave personal doubts sometimes. If you often get grey and black (in clouds, for example) you are certainly worrying – probably about money or your home. You may feel someone is not being completely honest with you. Try taking this further and asking questions, but it may be best to leave things to another day when your own mind is more positive and sunny – the colours should react similarly. However, never assume dark colours are automatically a bad omen. You are probably just being overanxious.

WHAT DO I DO NEXT?

Once you have experienced this glimpse of activity in the crystal, you can take it a little bit further. As you contemplate the colour hues in the glass, try stepping back in your mind's eye and asking questions that concern you. The colour often does relate to the department of life that you are most interested in, but almost any of the colours above can be consulted in an oracular fashion.

What I mean is this: once you perceive the light or colour, mentally ask about any issues you have, for work, for your family, for business, for love. If the colour or light visibly lightens, brightens or widens in the glass, you're being given a positive direction. Follow your inclinations and expect good results. As soon as you see any changes, ask a little further. You can try making this more personal either by asking about someone, or even imaging their face right into the centre of the colour in the glass itself. Place the person in your glass world, and look for any changes. If you perceive any sense or feeling of movement – especially upwards – in the glass, the answers are positive. You may also become vaguely aware of sounds or smells. This is giving more information.

You may find the colours or lights eventually trigger a genuine sense of self-hypnosis. At this stage, ask your inner being for any information relating to the things most on your mind. The crystal is inducing a trance-like state. Take the opportunity to look deeply into things that you will now understand clearly and wisely. This feeling may last a moment or for many minutes, but once you feel heavy or tired, imagine counting yourself upwards from twenty to one, and when you reach one, you will be smiling, feeling lighter and have a normal consciousness again.

COLOURED CLOTHS

In keeping with the meaning of the colours, try selecting special coloured cloth backdrops to provoke the crystal ball to focus on particular questions. Use a pink cloth if you are interested in seeing into your love life, yellow for questions relating to study or business, and green if you are worried about someone's health. This way, you are directing the energy of the crystal, and it will be able to synchronize with your thoughts very quickly. You may still see myriad colours in the glass, even with such dominant under-cloths. Experiment and see how you can best work with your crystal ball; remember, it has a mind (or an eye) of its own.

THE CLAIRAUDIENT'S FIRST RESPONSE

If you are a more audio-aware person, you may find that your sense of vision in the crystal is always subordinate to a sense of sounds. You may experience an actual sight – or feeling – of the colours, or just some prisms of light which may spark off the most wonderful panoply of audio messages. Many of us are more like this. Use the crystal as your receiver, and don't be afraid to pick it up and even close your eyes to listen to the messages that will literally pour forth into your mind's inner ear. You may receive very sophisticated messages this way, and perhaps even hear sounds like music, a baby crying, bird-song, some-one's voice, traffic or the seashore. For you, the crystal ball may always work in this way, but if you're lucky, eventually the sounds may be accompanied by visions inside your head of very complex pictures. It is no failure, however, if the sounds always dominate. Just enjoy listening to them.

Chapter 5

More complex visions

As you begin to get results with your visions and the colours or lights start to come with greater freedom, you will trigger off a more developed response. Richer images will ultimately come; you will find you have unlocked your deeper communicative powers with the astral plane.

You might like to think of this important step as a meeting with your own inner spirits or guides. Conceive of this as, perhaps, a manifestation of your unconscious being, or of an awareness of a world of other, more minute energies (such energies as are harnessed in magical ritual), or of communion with spirits in whichever way you imagine this to be. We all experience this a little differently, and with varying emphasis. We will consider this issue more closely in the last chapter, but for the moment, think of your more sophisticated visions as a communication line which you have established with the astral plane, or (if you like) with your own personal guardian angels. I like to imagine it is the most enigmatic core of my undiscovered, or uncharted, self. As such, it is the invitation to greater self-knowledge over many years, and a greater attentiveness to the invisible pulse beats, and the dream world, all around us. It is a chance to comprehend a subtler, less personal, intelligence.

WHEN WILL THIS HAPPEN?

The first occasion for reaching this – partly self-hypnotic state – may come within your first or second crystal gazing session. Suddenly, you may find you have achieved a transformation – like tripping a switch – and that colours or vague lights have become much clearer, giving way to a sudden swirl of shapes or pictures. You will probably find this happens without you having to try too hard, and before you have even realized what is happening. The crystal ball has, quite literally, started operating as a television set.

Don't panic if it takes you several sittings, or even several months, to reach this phase: it is strongly related to how readily you are able to let your conscious mind 'recede'. Often, those who have trouble getting to sleep quickly also take longer to reach this dreamy, crystal-aware state. Or you may be someone who, like me, doesn't even give in to drugs or painkillers readily: your mind wants to be in charge all the time! Don't give up, but do try to give yourself plenty of time, and enjoy the process. In the meantime, your mind's eye will probably continue to see images inside your head, prompted by the current of the ball. Consider these as being just as important as if they were in the ball itself.

RICHER IMAGES AND DEEPER MEANINGS

Let us ponder the images you may be receiving. Below is a list of sorts, but it isn't comprehensive, because a scryer working well can receive as many different types of visions as there are dreams and pictures – impossible to calculate. Take the images here as a prompt, and consider the associative significance of your own ideas as personally as you wish.

Most often, early symbols will come in groups that are quite simple – fruits, flowers, faces, and even familiar spaces. You may also see small animals or tiny objects. Here are some that I have either experienced myself or discussed with others who have seen them quite clearly.

- **Fruits** such as apples, grapes, stone fruits and, especially, berries usually indicate energy or time well spent, either on a project or with a person. If it's single in number, a new adventure is just starting or about to unfold. If you smell anything while you experience this image, you're breaking out of a stagnant phase of your life into a blossoming period.

- **Flowers**, particularly roses of any colour, or pretty flowers on single stems. These usually presage invitations or new beginnings in a love affair. Posies are very good omens for love, and pots or gardens full of flowers indicate emotional growth and a blossoming time in love.

Concentrate on these images and ask questions if you have someone in mind to ask about; if the image moves or becomes brighter or clearer, matters are steadily improving. If the flowers fade or vanish, the love matters you have asked about are problematic. A garden on its own indicates an important party or social gathering.

✿ **Insects** such as ants, ladybirds or bees. These are seen, perhaps surprisingly, by a lot of people. They seem to come up in the crystal when there has been a period of intense work, or when there is a need for a period of industry. They often indicate work and success, as well as the need to work in tandem with someone else – a partner or loved one. If you see an insect in the crystal, you can expect, soon, to be very focused on your business life, and study, too, perhaps.

✿ **Birds** are very frequently observed messengers for crystal scryers. Small birds (robins, wrens, finches, sparrows and so on) suggest activity and the need to be very steady in what you want to do. They often represent excitement, sometimes accompanied by nervousness. See what other images follow or precede the birds. If you see a large bird – a raven, crow, hawk, or owl, for instance – you have a weighty decision to make. You need all your wits about you, and must decide alone. These birds don't mean things will go badly, merely that you must be wise in the next few weeks.

- **Books** appear regularly for me and other people. They usually imply there is information available that you haven't yet 'read' or researched in your life, and can also suggest study or the need to learn something. When you see a ring and then a book, a marriage is going to take place shortly.

- **Landscapes** such as a forest scene, or countryside stretching out before you. If this is not a recognizable landscape, it is probably symbolic. A forest indicates a feeling of personal entrapment which you need to escape from; rolling countryside indicates a journey before you – even a personal voyage of discovery. Look deeply at the image, and see if you can probe it a little. Are there any recognizable features in it – a river, a cottage, an animal? You need to think about this at your leisure – it is a very important image to get.

- **Seascapes** mean you have a choice. These images sometimes indicate a connection with the sea: someone who comes from overseas, or a meeting by water. I have had this so often in my life, and now live in a house beside a river. However, it could also be a hint concerning your unconscious mind. If you see – or hear – the sea, your dreams are worth paying special attention to. Your deeper consciousness has messages to give you, and you are trying to sort through enormously important issues that will affect your whole life for some time to come. The sea is momentous. Pay attention to any other images that come with, or after, this important vision.

And now let us consider some groups ...

Travel is indicated by a car, boat or plane. A relationship in difficulty will be heralded by sharp objects, such as knives, scissors or broken glass. A box or a closed door indicates confinement or an obstacle, whereas an open door portends a sudden change of experience, as do crossroads. Jewellery suggests a new intimacy or confirmation of a bond, whereas a ring means a relationship is about to develop, but a pearl can indicate tears still to be cried before the direction of a love is settled. A basket, angel or fairy indicate help from an unexpected source, whereas an arrow, a feather, a horse or an implement of writing tell of news on its way. Musical instruments suggest a need to sit down and talk with someone, to find peace between you.

As you will understand from this process, much of what you receive will take the form of a symbolic thought process. This is especially true if you have asked a question about something or someone from the crystal. It is largely for you to look for connections between the events in your life and the pictures you are receiving; but there will be times when you see something quite different, too.

REAL ACTIONS

You may find that you are suddenly looking at a miniature movie – this can be rather like a déjà vu experience. The more adept you become at crystal gazing, the more often you will trip this 'camera' into action, literally photographing events that have been, or that are to come. Sometimes they will be like a snapshot: analyse the images carefully, as if you're looking at a photograph. It will show a scene that was important and formative – where events may have changed as a result of it. If it is the future – which you will deduce from its unfamiliarity – look at it carefully and try to recognize issues that are coming to a head around you. It may easily be that the solution to some stresses that you are experiencing currently can be resolved in the frame in front of you.

Sometimes, you will actually see moving pictures. This can be a replay of something that was, again, formative – an important (and usually recent) event; but it is just as possible that it is an event that will occur shortly – something that will be of vital significance. Look carefully, without panic, and see if you can understand what you are being shown. It is pointing you towards a defining moment.

DREAMS AND DÉJÀ VU

Using a crystal will often allow you to experience more informative and visionary dreams, so that you become more at one with your dream state. You may find that, after using the crystal for just a few weeks, you are able to direct your dream state to give you answers, help you understand others' points of view, and even to expand images you have had in the crystal. Simply put some rose or neroli oil on your pillow, close your eyes, think of an image you have experienced in the crystal ball, and count down from twenty with the image in your mind, relaxing your whole body from your toes gradually up to your head. Count slowly: you will sleep quickly and well, and find that your dreams pick up where the crystal left off, giving you much more information and even a story about what you have seen. Keep a notebook beside the bed to jot down things that are important, if you half-wake after a dream; details are easy to forget when you are fully wake in the morning.

You will also find that déjà vu often occurs once you start talking to your crystal ball. This is simply a response to increased awareness of your psychic strengths and gifts. You should enjoy the feeling – although it may not tell you anything too important. That is more likely to come from the crystal and your dreams.

PAST AND PRESENT

If you wish to scry with particular emphasis on the past, the present or, of course, the future, you must direct your crystal gazing session to this effect: as you start gazing, count yourself downwards from twenty, asking for images from your (possibly recent) past that have been significant for your present. Perhaps they are things you would like to see have a different outcome. Keep directing the crystal to reveal the past and, when you have been shown the scenes or pictures that unlock this riddle, move on in your mind, asking for the present: direct the ball to show you what is most important in the here and now. If there are things that have gone awry, try to imagine a better solution, envisaging peace or a happier ending. Finally, start counting backwards, from twenty again, and ask for a glimpse of the future that will help you to develop the present wisely: it may be about a relationship or concerning an important decision you have to make. Be firm with the ball: ask it to tell you exactly what you need to know. You will be amazed at how far you can take this, always directing the flow of time. To move forwards, you might wish to imagine a month showing on the calendar. For instance, you might ask how things will be at work, or in your house, or with your lover, by Christmas, or when the roses are blooming in the coming summer, and so on. This way, you can move forwards in time, like a camera panning through the future. It is a fantastic experience, and you will find you can do it quite readily, once you have mastered the knack of letting your visions flow.

READING FOR OTHERS

It is natural that you will want to try reading for other people; and this you can do, providing you are not twisting their willingness. Never force a reading on someone who is wary or reluctant. They have a right to their privacy. You also need to remember that to read for another person requires a control of your own ego: make sure you are wanting to be genuinely helpful, and not manipulative.

However, assuming someone comes to you to ask for a reading, the way to proceed is to get them to hold the ball for a few moments in the warmth of their hands, and then to lightly wipe it over to remove finger marks. It will help if you select a cloth that is different from the one you use for yourself: light mauve is a good colour for a third party, and a darker shade of purple (but not too dark) will help unlock their own psychic current along with yours. Now, ask them to count backwards from twenty to one, eyes closed, and you should share this process with them. *You* must ask for the direction of past or future –

the crystal is *your* tool. You should soon be experiencing images for them, and can interpret as you go. Sometimes it helps to ask a few questions of them, to clarify the symbolic meaning. Not infrequently, both of you will be able to see some shared images, especially of colours.

Don't read for anyone (including yourself) if they are especially depressed or unwell: the images may be particularly negative, and not a good indicator of what is ahead. This would distress everyone concerned. Also, don't do it too often, either for somebody else or for yourself; the more often you gaze, the shorter distance ahead you can see. Once a month should be more than enough for a personal reading, and, for others, every three months is good. More often than this and you end up seeing very little of the future indeed: the 'eye' looks only as far as the next session.

Never read for someone else if you feel unsure whether it's a good idea: you may be picking up signals that something is amiss. Follow your instinct. Also, never feel pushed into it: you can give very little if you feel you are being pressured, and you may suggest leaving it until another day. If you are worrying about something negative in the person who wants the reading, you can always say you are tired or not 'up to scratch' today, and ask them to respect your disinclination, leaving it for another occasion. You are probably right to leave it alone sometimes!

Chapter 6

Taking it further

B Y THE TIME YOU READ this chapter you will have had at least a few sessions gazing into your crystal. Perhaps you have some feelings about what more you would like to try to do with it. You may already have a view about whether using the ball affects you in any way. Many people have discovered that they're more restful and at peace after scrying; some of my friends who are experienced scryers, feel that their overall health has improved – that they are less susceptible to colds and bugs than other people – and that using the ball is instantly calming and helps to strengthen and focus the mind. I wonder if you have noticed this yet?

Much more attention has now, quite rightly, been given to crystals and their properties. It is my intention here, to look at other ways you can use your crystal ball, and combine it with other crystals to harness different energies from them, for healing and spiritual dimensions beyond scrying.

'PLAYING' WITH THE BALL

Of course, the ball is not a toy: you must always treat it with respect and love. But there are many things you can do with the crystal which will entice a greater affinity between you both, and also extend the range of activity the ball can contribute to. Think of it as a living being – a child-like spirit that wants affection and attention. Place fresh, scented blooms around it sometimes. Take it, occasionally, to some newly mown grass and let it 'breathe' there. And, perhaps most importantly, charge it up with energy like a battery – this can be done by the moon's light.

To do this, you must fill the ball with light. Perhaps as often as once a month, on the night of a full moon, open your ball's 'eye' to the moon to drink up its sensitivities and visionary powers. Set it on a silken cloth on a window sill or table, where it will catch the moon's rays. If you have a secure garden or balcony, you could place the ball there, safely nestled in soft fabric. If you have a new venture starting in your life – a new job, relationship, house move, or some study, or even a major trip planned – you might prefer to do this 'charging' on a new moon, when you are encouraging the 'moon of new beginnings' to illuminate your crystal. After this, you will find a new, special energy level in your scrying.

You might also like to let the sun greet the ball sometimes – especially on days of heightened solar energy. Midsummer sunrise is a good time for the crystal to be out of doors and drink in the sun's warmth, as is sunrise on Yule (21 December). Leave the ball for a few days after this before you read with it – it will give the new energy a chance to magnetize the ball. Do be careful when you are placing the ball in sunshine – it has the properties of a magnifying glass, and can burn whatever is under it, so place it on a heat-resistant surface, and don't leave it long in strong sunlight. Dawn's rays are quite sufficient.

RELEASING SPIRITS AND GUARDIAN ANGELS IN THE BALL

I have spoken in the previous chapter about spirits in the crystal, and it is worth recounting here some thoughts about spirit presences. Whatever else they may be, they have an intelligence and identity all their own – whether they are a part of your own inner self, or a separate entity. You will have your own ideas about this, and I am not going to try to debate which might be right here. I do believe, however, that the crystal manifests a side of our spirit being – whether of ourselves, or something 'other' – which we should respect and work with to get the best from our ball. You might like to imagine the spirit essence of the crystal as a kind of good helper – an angelic presence – which stands close to you while you see. Treat this essence with reverence and not too much scepticism! Their compliance will make your life and your visionary power stronger. If you always pour white light into, and around, the ball with your mind's eye (as well as real light and candles) before you start scrying, you will keep any negative input out – whether it is from your subconscious mind, or not. When the ball is in resting mode, you could enhance the magical spirit-feeling of the ball by placing it with some nice oils, rose petals or other flowers, and soft fabrics. You might also place crystals around your ball, to kindle a relationship of strength and affinity among them.

OTHER CRYSTALS AND YOUR CRYSTAL BALL:
SHAMANIC WISDOM

Many ancient teachings suggest there is a co-relationship between all crystals and stones; they are entities by themselves, and are also affiliated to one another. Shamans invested stones and crystals with healing powers and magical properties, and combined them with herbs and chanting to intensify their energy. Placed beside your glass crystal, you can borrow the information and 'voice' of other crystals to amplify your own glass ball. You can also try this with gemstones, which will add colour and imagination to the crystal, as well as creating a special energy field.

- **Rose crystal (rose quartz)** Place a rose crystal with your ball to infuse it with love, and to work healing powers through your emotional life. Rose quartz is associated with the heart chakra, and has a steady, colour-healing energy that will add information to your crystal ball. Keeping a rose crystal around you may help you to unlock your emotional capacity, to feel, articulate and experience love, and to drop premeditations which often hinder a love bond. Stroking rose crystal allows an alteration in your love vibration, so that you can forgive (yourself, as well as others), and helps to heal a wounded heart or a crushed ego. Placing it next to your ball – in the cloth, perhaps, or beside it on a table – will amplify the effect of the rose crystal, like viewing it through a magnifying glass. It also persuades your crystal ball to be wise and informative in matters of love. Have both your ball *and* a rose crystal beside you at night if you are coping with disappointment in love, or if you have had an argument with a loved one.

- **Fluorite crystals** These are very pretty, and are sometimes called Chinese fluorite though they come from many countries, including England. They are available in a variety of hues – mauves and purples through to pinks, greens and yellows. They usually have a precise, geometric shape – like a cube. Use them according to colour to add energy to your crystal ball – a green will help you to find out about health issues, whereas mauve will help to give your ball extra psychic strengths. Generally, a fluorite is a good choice of crystal to put near your ball as its energy is gentle and unobtrusive, so it won't interfere with the 'eye' itself.

- **Smoke quartz crystals** These are a brownish or greyish colour, and are very soothing to hold and work with. They are good to use if you are coming through a demanding time, when you have been overworked or feel 'burn-out' coming on from trying to balance too many disparate things. Simply sitting with your crystal and a smoke quartz together will regularize your breathing and help you to relax. If you work a reading with a smoke quartz beside you, you will soon see an end to a long period of relentless pushing. If you feel tired from reading for someone else, try placing the smoke crystal under your pillow, to recharge your own vitality.

PRECIOUS STONES AND HEALING

Some people believe that the powers of gems are derived from the colours, which excite a change of key in our moods. Or, perhaps the very slight variations in chemical composition of the gems – which result in considerable differences in the way the light enters the stones, emitting the different colours we perceive – interact powerfully with the human body, which is a composite structure of different minerals. Impulses are transmitted from the brain along the spinal cord, affecting our nerve impulses; in this way, our thoughts, emotions, creative ideas and feelings are a sophisticated chemical response, linking mind and body through the nervous system. Gemstones, with their subtly different refractive powers, may influence the light and chemical signals in our bodies; certainly, we all react strongly to the appearance, power and feel of different gems, and we all react individually. There is a lineage of teaching from peoples of ancient times to the modern day, which is interested in the way that over time, when gemstones are in contact with our body and spirit, exerting specific energy fields, they can manifest profound and significant changes in us. This is the origin of birthstones – the idea that individual signs have particular needs.

Try using gems with your crystal ball. Here is a guide to using them both on their own and with the ball.

- **Rubies** are governed by the Sun and are recommended when the nerves feel frayed or when physically fatigued. Place near the ball when reading for someone who is either concerned about their good name, or is suffering a lack of confidence about their personality.

- **Emeralds** are co-ruled by Mercury and Venus, and are perfect for curing mental burn-out, or if the liver has been inflamed. They empower the intellect, making them good for educational success. Place with the ball for mental clarity and focus.

- **Sapphires** are co-ruled by Jupiter and Saturn. They help cure chest complaints, and make us naturally more aware of staying scrupulously clean, helping sufferers of any skin condition that is minimized by good cleansing rituals – acne, for example, or even dandruff. Use sapphires when you need to organize yourself better. With the crystal ball, they boost the capacity to work hard.

- **Diamonds** are ruled by Venus. They are a fertility aid and a spur to creativity – especially literary. Diamonds are good for healing bone maladies. Place with your ball to magnify the strength and durability of a love relationship – if someone is going abroad, for instance.

- **Amethysts** are governed by the Moon and Neptune, and boost psychic energies and intuition. They help to heal persistent wounds and blood pressure problems, and also promote strong dreams. Use them with the crystal ball when you want to intensify the visions, and wear one at your throat if you want to speak in an inspirational way. Placed near the crystal, they may encourage sounds to come from the ball.

- **Pearls and moonstones** belong to the Moon, and help women to exude their best individual allurements! They help to deal with over-sentimentality and melancholia, and can remedy a slow metabolism and stomach ailments. Placed by the crystal ball, they amplify the sounds that come from it. Pearls may lead the ball to tell of the marriage state.

Placing gems or crystals near the crystal ball will magnify the powers of both, and set up a healing atmosphere. Sleep with them in the room to see how they best interact with your body chemistry. They will also help you to work well with the best and most positive spirit presences that are personal to you.

LAST IDEAS FOR YOUR CRYSTAL BALL

We are now in the realm of your own explorations. Volumes could be written abut the possibilities you have in front of you with your crystal ball, but these ideas are really an invitation to you to set your imagination free. You might try these ideas for yourself:

- **Transmit messages to a friend who has a crystal ball.** Use it like a telephone wire, to send a simple message or picture to someone else you know who has a crystal ball. Agree on a time and 'tune in' together, seeing if you can pick up on each other's thoughts. It is an excellent exercise for developing your psychic abilities.

- **Meet your spirit guide.** For you, this may be an ancestor (perhaps a grandparent you adored), a shamanic spirit, or even a guardian angel. Spray a little rose-scented spray before you begin, to open the channel to positive entities, and then imagine yourself right into the heart of the ball, using light and candles to create a powerful prism effect. Here, you can use your 'eye' to see what is normally out of focus. Ask your spiritual guide or guides to take you by the hand. Be positive and you will have nothing to fear. You may actually find you can see your guide. This will bring you into closer contact for the future, and you can explore this at your leisure.

✪ **Try astral travel.** As you sit in front of your crystal ball, use benzoin incense or room spray, and count yourself backwards from twenty, as you usually do. This time, imagine a light feeling spreading upwards from your feet, and vividly feel the light entering your chakras, or energy points: ankles, knees, lower spine, belly button, heart, 'third eye', and the top of your head. At the tip of your head, ask that you float free, to come back whenever you wish to, then open your eyes into the crystal ball, and look where you're travelling to. It may be a place in your past, or a country where someone you love is at present. It will feel more three-dimensional than usual gazing: you will feel a physical 'waftiness', as though you are floating. When you have had enough and you want to come back, imagine that a string of light is leading you back by your belly button, until you are aware that you are sitting in your own room. It takes a little practice but is an amazing feeling when you master it. If you find you can't manage it, don't worry. Not everyone can let go of the present, and that is fine. You may be someone who likes to be in control just a little too much for astral travel. Try something else.

✪ **See a wish come true.** Sit in front of the crystal ball with sharp scents such as cypress, pine or citrus, and try to imagine putting a particular vision *into* the ball – like the reverse of reading. This is like creating your own future – seeing a picture in the ball that you would like to happen: a kiss, a forgiveness, a successful outcome, a reunion, a graduation – really, anything you want to see come true in the future. By continually projecting it into the glass, you are directing your future. If you do this beneficently – don't ever wish anything mean onto another person – you will gently make inroads on what your future will actually be. This, I believe, is one of the best uses of both your imaginative power, and of the crystal ball. Stick at it ...

- ☼ **Use the crystal ball to create positive energy**, and as the nucleus of your 'bright-white-light' thoughts. Imagine bright lights encircling your ball, and then showering the room (even your whole house) with brilliant light. Imagine only good things will come to you, and that every tricky obstacle can be overcome with determination. This is a wonderful use of the ball, where it becomes a little personal moon in your home. Borrow its vibrancy often.

- ☼ **Aspire to a generous, higher consciousness.** Whenever you have had a disagreement with another person, or are just at odds with their ideas, use the ball to try to 'see' their viewpoint. Think vividly of the person as you sit in front of the ball with your eyes closed, and quietly direct the ball to help you see what they see. Think yourself into their head, and look out from behind their eyes, then gaze at the crystal to feel what they feel. You may be able to reach a wonderful level of compromise by understanding their viewpoint like this, and the ball will also act as an inversion – a mirror, if you like. As if by a little bit of magic, they, too, will understand a little of what *you* see. Amity may now be possible.

- **And finally: keep a diary.** The best way to see your progress is to create a scrying journal, with the date, the weather and the moon phase, along with the oils, scents or music you used. This way you will find what works best, and, of course, you're keeping a record. Sometimes, looking back, it will astonish you when you remember what you have seen. You will find you really are quite clairvoyant!

WHAT DOES THE FUTURE HOLD FOR YOUR CRYSTAL BALL?
This little book has hopefully been an introduction to the pleasures of crystal ball gazing. If you and your crystal ball are working well together, you could be at the beginning of a long love affair! Don't hurry: enjoy the whole experience. Your visions will be different from mine – from anyone's. You are unlocking a deeper part of yourself, and the journey will be fascinating. Good luck, and may your globe be filled with the future visions you wish for!

Resources

If you want to learn more (and you will, won't you?), here are some suggestions for further reading, and some suppliers who can provide you with items to expand your crystal gazing.

Further reading

Chakra Workbook: Rebalance your body's vital energies, Pauline Wills. Gateway 2000

Color and Crystals: A Journey through the Chakras, Joy Gardner. Crossing Press 1988

The Crystal Ball, Sybil Ferguson. Red Wheel/ Weiser 1980

Crystal Balls and Crystal Bowls: Tools for Ancient Scrying and Modern Seership, Ted Andrews. Llewellyn 1995

Crystal Gazing and Clairvoyance: The Secrets of the Future Revealed Through the Ancient Art of Scrying, John Melville. Aquarian Press 1987

The Crystal Wisdom Kit: Cast the crystals for healing, insight and divination, Stephanie Harrison and Barbara Kleiner. Connections 1997

Exploring Scrying: How to Divine the Future and Make the Most of it, Ambrose Hawk. New Page 2001

Scrying for Beginners: Tapping into the Supersensory Powers of Your Subconscious, Donald Tyson. Llewellyn 1997

10 minute Crystal Ball: Easy Tips for Developing Your Psychic Powers, Skye Alexander. Fair Winds Press 2002

Suppliers

American Pearl
americanpearl.com
For pearls in various forms

Aqua Sapone
soap.it
For a wide range of soaps, as well as tips for making your own scented vinegar

Bath Time Cape May
bathtimecapemay.com
Suppliers of quality bath and body products, including a variety of triple-milled soaps

bestcrystals.com
Has a full range of crystals and gemstones

Incensemania
The Online Incense Store
incensemania.site.yahoo.net
Suppliers of all kinds of incense products, including benzoin incense sticks

Ladyhawk's Treasures
ladyhawkstreasures.com
For a wide range of mind body spirit products, including gems and crystals

Neal's Yard Remedies
nealsyardremedies.com
Suppliers of a full range of essential oils

vitabeads.com
For gemstones and semi-precious stones

INDEX

ABOUT THE AUTHOR

Titania Hardie is Britain's most famous White Witch. Through her mother's guidance she nurtured her own psychic abilities and developed a deep affinity for understanding nature and harnessing its power to enhance lives and wellbeing. Titania has a degree in psychology and has trained in parapsychology and horary astrology. She also has degrees in English literature and romantic studies. She has made hundreds of television appearances around the world, and has received widespread national newspaper and magazine coverage.

Her previous titles include *Hocus Pocus*, *Titania's Fortune Cards* and *Dreamtime*. Her books have sold over 1.2 million copies worldwide. In 2002, Boots the Chemist (UK) successfully launched *Titania Hardie Beauty Spells*, an exclusive collection of magic and bath and beauty products.

ACKNOWLEDGEMENTS

The author gratefully acknowledges all at Eddison Sadd and especially Ian Jackson and Robert at PFD.

EDDISON • SADD EDITIONS

EDITORIAL DIRECTOR	Ian Jackson
EDITOR	Katie Ginn
PROOFREADER	Peter Kirkham
ART DIRECTOR	Elaine Partington
MAC DESIGNER	Malcolm Smythe
PRODUCTION	Sarah Rooney and Charles James